AMANDA WRIGHT

Mom Works

Lose the guilt. The art of balancing business and family.

This book was professionally typeset on Reedsy.
Find out more at reedsy.com

Contents

Introduction

Every person has some knowledge they can pass on to others, so when I thought about why I wanted to write this book, I decided that even if I am not the very best mother in the world, even if I am not an expert at productivity and time management, and even if I am also not a professional organizer, I am those things to my family. I have struggled, I have despaired, I have found balance and I have discovered ways of finding joy in the abundant mess that is life sometimes. I can share my experiences and what I have learned from being a very busy mama, business owner and personal assistant (to my kids!), and as you know, the list goes on and on of all the hats we wear as mamas who also have a career.

I spent many years feeling alone, and sad sometimes, to the point of depression, but what did I have to be so down about? I started a graphic design business that was growing and paying my salary. I discovered the type of work that truly fulfills my creative side AND my super detailed oriented side. I gave birth to two beautiful, mostly healthy, children. I had a family who loved me and showed up in my life. I had some pretty great friends too. So what was causing me so much distress? To the outside world, I had all the things I wanted and should be grateful. I felt like I had to push down those feelings of unrest and anxiety, as well as the negative self-talk, that I wasn't good enough. But, I never told anyone. I never put a voice to my thoughts and struggles. After all, I am a strong, independent woman. I can handle all of this and I should be happy doing it, shouldn't I?

However, my internal voice said I wasn't being the best mother, I wasn't managing all of my business tasks perfectly, and on top of that, I was out of shape and tired ... always so very tired. I looked in the mirror and didn't recognize the person before me. The joy that once easily poured out of me was replaced by stress, sharp tones, constantly telling my kids I can't, I have to work, then resented the work that I loved so much. I was more than burning the candles at both ends, I barely slept, I ate whatever I could shove in my face and floated from one task to the next, never feeling truly engaged in any area. I was literally uninspired in all facets of my life.

I felt so drained, as I was stretched to the max being a mama and business owner, that I stopped feeling present in the moment. When I was with my kids, I was thinking about the work tasks that I hadn't completed yet. When I was working, I was constantly thinking about my kids. Did I tell them I loved them when I dropped them off, did I put the extra water in my daughter's backpack, does my son have his jacket, do they know how great I think they are? Do my kids see the real me? Or do they see this tired, ragged person that appears to be utterly unhappy and hiding in her closet crying. Yes, I had special crying places to hide from my kids. Sound familiar yet?

I felt like I lost my identity as a person and was just a mom or business owner. I didn't feel like me, and I wasn't doing anything to change it. Self-care was not a word in my vocabulary. I once felt like I was a very strong person, but I was reduced to a crying, anxious, depressed version of myself, allowing my inner voice to convince me I was failing at it all.

But do you know what the real truth was? I just had some bad habits, I was a little disorganized in how I arranged my day, I failed to plan ahead some days, and I never took time for myself to recharge.

The truth was I was juggling too many roles and responsibilities and there was no balance, just what felt like chaos. My mental load was at an all time high and I had no coping mechanisms in place to handle all the changes that occur in parenthood, as children grow, and in business, as it grows and changes. I realized that I am not a bad mother. I was never failing my kids. My business and my talents as a designer were growing, but in order for me to embrace it all, and truly enjoy my life again, I knew I had to take a step back and really examine my current state of being. I couldn't keep going the way I was because my children deserve the best version of me. I had to find a better way to do life and I knew I couldn't do it alone. Although it is true that seeking balance and harmony is a life-long journey, it is attainable in the here and now. I went on a journey to discover my identity at this stage in my life, how to balance all that was important to me, how to be the best mother I could and thrive in my career. Everyone's story is different. Everyone's struggles are unique. Everyone experiences highs and lows in life. But you don't have to do it alone. My book will just scratch the surface of what you can attain online, in books, in magazines, in small groups, in community, that you can use to help you grow, seek balance, and find contentment and joy in your daily life. My hope is that this book will inspire you to do just that.

If you have ever felt guilt about how you juggle your career and parenthood, never feeling like you're quite getting it right, then please read on. You can lose the guilt and master the art of balancing business and family.

Chapter 1: Self-Exam

I think the first step in implementing any kind of change is always the hardest. It's acknowledging that the way things are isn't working and making the decision to do something about it. Oftentimes people just keep going, doing the same things they've always done, hoping life will magically get better. Isn't that the literal definition of insanity, yet so many fall into its trap. What I discovered is the only way to ensure positive change is to live with intention. At first I didn't realize I wasn't living with intention. On paper, my life sure seemed like I was, but in reality I was mindlessly floating from one task and project to the next, trying to get through this week or that deadline. I always said next week or next month I'm going to sit down and get better organized, but I didn't for quite a long time. So, once I decided I was ready for change and motivated to take action, I knew I had to really take the time to analyze where I was at currently. You might be thinking, where am I going to get more time to do that?

I thought the same thing at first, but then I realized I had to solve this problem like anything else I do in my life. You think through the components of the problem, you research possible solutions, you read up on the subject matter, you find inspiration, and you take action on what seems to make the most sense for your circumstance. So, in my downtime (I know, laughable concept), such as when I was in the shower, driving home from dropping kids off, in the ummm, bathroom, basically wherever I could get a moment alone, I would use the time to think. I've always been such an analytical person, so this part was easier than I expected, but facing the realities was a bit harder.

Side note: If you haven't already, I strongly urge you to grab a notebook as you begin this process with me and read on. It doesn't have to be a fancy journal, just something you can collect all your thoughts in together, so you have a point of reference for this journey. This notebook will become your life manual, the guide to changing your life for the better. It doesn't have to be fancy or super organized, but it will be a place to capture all the things in your mind and give a voice to those nagging feelings you carry around. You will use it to write out thoughts, hopes, dreams, goals, prayers and gratitude. You can use it to even create vision boards.

I took a hard look at myself, my current life circumstances - the good, the bad, the difficult - and examined the sheer amount I put on myself each day. I was seriously expecting a miracle to happen almost daily to complete the endless to-do's on my list. I asked myself, would I expect this type of workload out of another person? The answer was easily no. Just because I could produce under the chaos doesn't mean it was all quality in every area either. I did have a lot of miracles in those days, somehow keeping my head above water, but I wasn't living well. After I spent several days just thinking and analyzing it all in my head, I pulled out a notebook and began writing down all my responsibilities, separating it by business, housework and children. I started thinking about how much time I spent in these different areas and could easily deduce why I had zero time left for myself. And I wondered why I felt so unhappy? It was staring me in the face.

I was over scheduled, overworked and quite frankly overwhelmed, but I kept bottling it up until it spilled out in ways that made me ashamed. I hate to admit it, but I know a lot of mothers have been where I have - losing patience and raising my voice at my kids and not for things that needed a sharp tone. I would cry and hate myself and ask for their forgiveness, but just do it all over again in a month's time when I hit my next breaking point. They were kids, just being kids, needing their loving, nurturing mama, not this overworked, haggard woman yelling at them to pick up their dirty clothes. I kept telling myself I could manage, but in reality I was just surviving. That's not the life I wanted for myself or my kids. I knew I was put on this earth to thrive. I was given gifts and talents, drive, determination, and dammit I am not weak and I was sick and tired of feeling weak.

During a particularly bad day, I heard a song by Lauren Daigle called, "Still Rolling Stones," and it spoke to my soul. I was tired of feeling defeated and she sang the words, "Rise up, rise up; All at once, I came alive," and I got chills. It was time I held my head up and started believing in myself again. It was time I rise up and take control of my life and not let it continue to pass me by. I was existing, not living. I told myself I am the same woman who went to design school at night and eventually became pregnant and quit her job at a great law firm. I was fierce and brave and I could be those things again. I had a child coming into the world but I knew I was called to find a career using my creative talents and helped start not one, but two businesses. The first did not work out and I never quit, I never gave up on myself, so why was I doing it now? What happened to the fire inside me and why did I let life extinguish it?

This prompted me to think back (and write down) how I did things before I had children and what my life was like. I thought about my mindset back then and I wrote down all the things I used to enjoy (like reading a book for fun!), hobbies I let go of, and activities that really brought me joy. I thought about what I wanted to bring back into my life. I knew I had to find a way to build time into my schedule for me or my identity as an individual would never come back in the foreseeable future and that was an important piece missing in the way I was living. I knew I needed to not only better myself to be a better mama and better at my job, but I also needed to love myself again and nurture the creative sides of my personality that brought me so much joy and purpose.

Over the course of many days I started reviewing where all my time went in much more detail. I asked myself what things aren't working? What is sucking too much time without being beneficial? What is stressing me out? What do I dread? What are the biggest challenges and obstacles standing in my way? Then I asked myself the opposite of all of those questions. What is working? What brings me peace and happiness? What can't I wait to do? What are the wonderful parts of my life that bring me fulfillment?

Chapter 2: Dream Big, Then Do Your Homework

After I analyzed and wrote out all of the good and bad things present in my daily life, I wanted to take it a step further. I knew I couldn't simply cut out the things I didn't like doing. It's never that simple, is it? What I needed to do was dream up what I wanted my life to be, just like I did all those years ago in my 20's. I needed to imagine what my life could be like so I could figure out how to get there. So I spent even more time thinking and journaling about what truly brings me joy and fulfillment in life. I thought about things I wanted to do that I hadn't done, like writing this book, learning to play golf, and attending as many major league baseball games as I could squeeze in. I wrote down all the wishes I had in my heart for my personal life and my children's. I thought about things I wanted to do for myself that I wasn't doing.

But I didn't stop there. I couldn't just dream about how our home life would be. I had to set goals for my personal career growth and for my business. I came up with many big goals and realized they were probably too broad, but don't worry about that for yourself. Just write it all down. Later, go back and analyze these goals. Any big goal or dream can be broken down into smaller goals and achieved in phases. I realized I needed to set realistic goals little by little so I could see progress. This is something I hadn't done in 10 years and I can't help but wonder how I even got to where I am without returning to this activity. I simply had to envision it all.

You might be wondering, "Ok, that's a lot of self-reflection, that's a lot of analyzing, that's a lot of dreaming, but what did you do with all of those discoveries? How do you even take action on that information and implement it into your life?"

What made the most sense to me was to do research, and a lot of it. My first degree was in Political Science, and no I am not directly using it, nor have I ever really, but I learned a lot of valuable lessons earning that degree that I have continued to apply to my life. A few major things were developing my analytical skills, my research skills, and my writing skills. Every single class required all of the above. I analyzed the topic, researched it to death, and developed my viewpoint for the papers and essays. Researching became my favorite part of the process and made everything that came after so much easier. So, I applied what I knew to this problem. How do I find myself again, how do I create balance, how do I structure my life to achieve what I want, to arrive at the conclusions where joy and success intersect?

Remember when I said at the beginning I am no expert in any particular area that I am writing about? Well, that is still true, but you know what, there are so many people that are. There are so many mamas that work struggling with the same exact things as you and me, and there are solutions. Not everything you read will be right for you, but you have to start somewhere. You need to find inspiration. You need to read things that inspire your soul.

I wrote down topics I thought would make the most sense to research (however in depth) and I would read as much as possible on these topics to formulate my response to the problems I discovered in my evaluation phase. You can find this information by reading books and blog articles in the areas you need to learn more about, or even listening to books and podcasts as you go about your day. The idea is to fill yourself up with knowledge on subjects you know you are lacking in to gain insight and understanding. Knowledge gives you power over your circumstances and will lead you in the direction you need to go. Your list may be shorter or longer than mine, but below are the areas I jotted down.

Self-Care

I've come to understand that self-care is just about anything that makes you feel more like yourself - it isn't just a massage or a bubble bath! For me, self-care does include those indulgences, but it's also curling up with a good book, going for a run on a beautiful day, watching an entire baseball game, sometimes in the middle of the day! Oh my word, the world might stop spinning if I don't work 12 hours a day! Wrong. The breaks I took, like golfing a half day once a month, or getting brunch with my girlfriends on a Tuesday, made me feel SO much better. I was enriched. My soul was fed by the things that bring me joy and because of it, I was even more motivated when I got back to my desk. My kids noticed my happier demeanor. There was and is, joy to be found in the everyday. Self-care doesn't end there though. One author I read totally spun self-care as a discipline, rather than indulgences. I saw her point. Self-care is also about knowing yourself, your limitations and setting boundaries for your own well-being. Sometimes that means ending the binge watching session so you can get some much-needed shut eye, or deciding not to attend a function because you really need the time for something else. Allowing yourself to say no sometimes is what you need. Self-care doesn't have to always be indulgences, but I don't think we can limit it to just doing the things that are good for us. As in everything, we need a balance between discipline, doing what's best for ourselves, and indulgences, doing things that bring joy.

Self-Love

Showing kindness and compassion to yourself, just like you do for others. This is one of the topics I needed to learn more about than most. Being a naturally selfless person, I didn't understand the detrimental impact of not loving myself, or the example I was giving to my children, especially my daughter. Self-love isn't selfishness or arrogance. It's loving the skin you're in and giving yourself grace. It's putting on the swimsuit and jumping into that pool with the kids. It's wearing shorts when you don't feel your most toned. It's forgiving yourself when you lose your cool. It's giving yourself grace when you're having a bout of sadness or a gloomy day. It's recognizing that you are human, but you are loved, you are worthy, you are valuable and you are here for so many beautiful reasons. I learned to never stop telling myself these things. I was made to shine and to prosper, but that will never happen if I don't first accept myself and love where I am. I do something wrong and now instead of wallowing in it, I embrace the mistake, learn from it and quickly let it go.

Exercise

We all know the importance of physical activity, so why is it the first thing to fall off a mother's list when life gets busy? I looked up so many at home workouts, but at the end of the day, I realized my one true love (in the exercise world that is!) is running. I began slowly and tried to make time for 30 minutes 3 times a week. As time progressed I knew this wasn't enough for me and realized I would succeed if I had encouragement from others and for the first time in my life, I joined a specialized fitness program that centers around group fitness classes that incorporated rowing, body weight exercises, weight lifting, and yes, running! It kicks my butt, literally, but the coach and the other people in the classes are encouraging and help you get through. The hardest part is just getting it scheduled. I realized for me, I am not super into fitness. I understand the importance of taking care of my body, the stress reducing benefits and the endorphins, but I didn't enjoy researching types of exercises and figuring out a schedule or routine to do on my own at home or in a gym. It just didn't interest me so joining group fitness classes where everything is planned out was right for me. I just had to show up. Thank God!

Nutrition

This is another area where I truly understand the value of it, but I just don't enjoy researching all the best types of foods and how I should eat them. Don't get me wrong, I love food, but I know myself and I know I would never adhere to any strict dieting plan. Instead I just try to eat as much lean meat, veggies and fruits as I can and save the sweets and treats for only a couple times per week. I enjoy pasta, rice, potatoes and bread, but my method was just eating those things in moderation. I didn't implement any set or strict regimen, I was just more mindful of what I ate and the extra pounds started melting away. It wasn't just the food though. It was exercising and starting to take better care of myself. There aren't any shortcuts in life no matter what people say. Small changes sustained over time will have big impacts.

Sleep

Oh my goodness, why did I think I could survive on just 4 or 5 hours of sleep a night for so many years. I would do that week after week and finally break down or get sick and be bed ridden. That would cause even more stress. I was so adamant about my children's sleep habits and ensuring they got the proper amount of hours in bed. I intently listened to the pediatrician's recommendations at every stage of their development and understood the importance of sleep, but why didn't I apply that to myself as well? The Sleep Foundation states that the average adult needs between 7-9 hours of sleep per night. 9 hours! Oh what a glorious day if I could sleep 9 whole hours. That felt like a luxury I just couldn't afford myself except maybe once a month on a Sunday. I started to think about how I actually felt after those nights that I did sleep longer. I felt refreshed, the brain fog lifted, I had energy, and to be very honest, I was a much nicer mommy. When I was reading up on how important sleep is, it was evident that I would become more productive with more rest.

I asked myself, how productive are you really at midnight trying to push through that to-do list? Drinking caffeinated drinks at 8pm to get a "second wind" was ludacris but I did it year after year and felt more tired and more stressed. I used excuses like, I'm a night owl, I'm more productive at night, but it was just a lie I told myself because I thought I needed to just keep going or I'd never get through everything that was expected of me. In reality, not sleeping enough was just contributing to my feelings of depression and allowing anxiety to rule the day, with a snippy undertone, I might add. Now, no matter what is going on, I'm allotting no less than 7 hours of sleep per day. I mean, it's science folks. We are just better performing people with more rest. I can do more in less time, because my brain is recharged. Imagine that.

Mindfulness

Now this is something I couldn't wait to read more on. I had heard so many positive things about being more mindful, but what exactly is it, what does it mean and how can I subscribe to that philosophy? The long and short of it is being mindful means we are fully present, aware of where we are, and what we are doing in the moment. For example, when you are spending time with your children, you are focused on your conversations with them. You are engaging and letting career, housework, etc. take a back seat in your brain. What I learned is that we already have the capacity to be mindful. This is inherently innate as human beings, so all we need to do to take advantage of it is practice. Sounds simple enough, and it should be! To practice mindfulness, all you need to do is take the time to create the space to think before you engage in the next activity of the day. Take just a few moments to center yourself, concentrate on what is coming next and clear the distractions to focus on what's ahead. Giving yourself these moments in between the endless to-do's of the day, can help you maintain a level of awareness and at the same time help you more fully engage. However, please remember that our brains will wander from time to time, you may get distracted or get off course, but the idea is to be able to immediately recognize when it's happening, adjust and refocus. We can only handle one thing at a time so remind your judgey inner voice to take a beat and fixate on the present moment. The more you practice bringing your mind back to this, you will notice reduced stress and heightened productivity.

Productivity

Back in 2011, when I was just beginning my new career path and starting my business, I read a book called "*Getting Things Done*" by David Allen. It was a game changer for me. The entire book is about stress-free productivity, time management, personal organization, and efficiency in your work life. Although I have implemented many of his tools into my life that still exist today, I won't pretend like I mastered all of the concepts he so perfectly laid out. What I wish I would have done was reread this book once I had two children under five while growing a business. I had forgotten so many valuable tips that had once helped me be the most productive version of myself. When I started on the journey I am on now, striving to better myself, I reread this insightful book and it helped me, once again, create structure in my work day, it helped me efficiently plan out my tasks, and ultimately reduce the stress with the demanding deadline schedule I had paired with the day to day of running a business. It gave me more time to focus and thus freeing my brain space up to give me periods of immense creativity that I fell in love with my design work all over again. I highly recommend this book and applying the practices you will learn within to not just your career. I began applying the principles to my home life and housework as well and I found myself with a more organized, clutter free home. And you know what? That uncluttered so much brain space for me that I was all around happier and more calm transitioning from one task to the next.

Chapter 3: Take Action & Make a Plan

Once I took the necessary time to evaluate where I'd been, where I wanted to go and researched all of the areas I felt I needed improvement, found encouragement and inspiration, I was ready to formulate a plan for my life. It was time to put into action all of the wonderful things I had learned and make them meaningful for me.

Now that we know that floating through or racing through life won't produce the results you are looking for, continually remember to slow down and live your life with intention. We've already discussed envisioning your dreams and goals and writing them down, but now it's time to hone in and focus on breaking down those goals into attainable action items. It's important to make these goals feel attainable so you continue the practice. You need to figure out a formula for what motivates you. Having a clear and specific vision will help you focus and mentally embrace what it will take to get there. Don't stop imagining and playing these dreams and goals in your mind. Create the vision board in your journal or on a wall you will see daily. Keep it at the forefront of your mind.

If you've been following along with me then you have already examined and evaluated what changes you need to make to attain what you want out of life. So, now is the time to make the conscious choice to act on them and put a plan into action. The best way to start that plan is with your schedule. Block out your day and include time for self-care, tending to your children, housework, after-school activities, and work time. You will need to set boundaries. There is simply no way around it. There are only 24 hours in the day and you need to plan for every one of them Monday-Friday. Give yourself a break and do not adhere to a strict schedule on Saturday and Sunday. You may want to schedule family activities or squeeze in an hour or two of work, but don't have any rules for those two days. Allow yourself some time for spontaneity and to just live.

Break your work time down into sections and start and end each work day with planning out tasks, grouping like tasks, and prioritizing. Schedule time that you remove all distractions, which most definitely includes mindless scrolling on social media. At this time your phone should be on silent/focus mode, notifications will be switched off, you will not be answering phone calls and text messages, and you will not be answering email just yet. Have a period of focused, top priority work time to allow your brain to hone in on the most important tasks that need to be completed that day. My suggestion is to do this type of work in the first few hours of the day. I find that before I let the weight of all the things weigh me down, I am so much more productive and creative, which is essential to design work. And for goodness sake, take a breakfast break, and take a lunch break. You are not a robot. You cannot sustain hour after hour after hour of extreme focused work. It doesn't work. I promise you I have tried time and again.

Once you block out your day, try your best to stick to doing those types of things in the time frames you set out. And when life happens, because we all know it will, take it easy on yourself. Practice mindfulness to get back to where you need to be once the distraction or life episode is wrapped up. Solve the problem or issue head on and then get back to it. There is no sense in stressing over deviating from the regularly scheduled programming because if you don't, that thing will just create angst, stress and anxiety that will in turn kill your productivity, steal your joy and just plain mess up the course of your day.

When things aren't going perfectly, I've learned to halt the negative self-talk and release the feelings of guilt of not getting everything right and not getting everything done I set out to do that day. Address the negative feelings immediately when they erupt. Take a focused pause and take back control of your emotions. Yes, I know that this is so much easier said than done, especially depending on what it is, but the more you engage in this type of intentional living, the better you will feel. I can promise you that. Recognize and even say out loud, I am only one person. I can only do one thing at a time. I can only be at one place at a time. Give yourself grace, take a deep breath, let go, and under no circumstances, compare yourself to what others are able to do and accomplish. Otherwise you are wasting the valuable time you do have on negative energy that does nothing for you or your loved ones. Instead, calm your mind and revert back to what the priority of the moment is. Clear the mental load, even for just the present moment so you can refocus.

It's important to regularly evaluate your schedule and list of to do-to's and responsibilities. Life is constantly changing and evolving and we have to be mentally prepared to change with it. Eliminate the things that drag you down or do not add to your life. Prioritizing how and where we spend our time is a skill so worth investing in developing. It takes drive and it takes intention, but you can do this too.

Do you remember when you were young and you colored pictures in a coloring book? Do you remember the feeling of a completed picture, with all the coloring in the lines, felt so good? I look back on it now and I think, for me at least, it felt good because it was fun to do, it was pretty to look at, it had structure, and I completed something. Wouldn't you know, this is the exact same way I feel now when I complete a design project, or reorganize the kitchen drawers or color code by wardrobe. Our minds crave beauty, organization, structure, and a sense of completion.

Please do not overlook the importance of creating structure and organizing your life, your home and your office. Put systems in place to achieve the results you desire. If it's heightening your productivity at work, adhere to a schedule as best you can and find methods that work for you to stay focused. If it's decluttering your home, find a system to remove things that don't belong or things that don't hold value by leaving an empty basket in all of the main areas of your home. As you go about your day and walk by something that doesn't belong in that room, simply place it in the basket so it's out of view and unclutters the area. Once a week, pick up the basket and distribute the items to their appropriate space or place the unwanted items in a bag or bin that you will donate to a local thrift store once you have enough items to warrant a trip.

The whole idea is to create organization and structure in every facet of your life to declutter what you see, what you feel and what is in your mind. If you can do that, you will find balance, you will find peace, and you will rediscover joy in your daily life because being a mama and pursuing your passions are what makes life worth living.

Conclusion

There is one last thing I want to share with you as you begin your own journey of seeking balance. It is something I believe I struggled with more than anything else, and that was asking for help. My innately independent spirit sometimes gave me the false impression that I was displaying weakness or a negative trait if I asked others for help. But I asked myself, what do I have to lose if I allow help? I couldn't come up with an answer. I had to let go of the idea that I could do it all and have it all, because that is a lie that will always leave you feeling defeated and less than. No one can do it all and have it all at the same time. Hire a maid, send the laundry out to be cleaned, hire a babysitter, hire a lawn maintenance company, buy the cake for the bake sale, lean on co-workers when it's appropriate, and please ask friends and family to pitch in sometimes. My parents are delighted when I allow them to help. When you lend a helping hand it gratifies the soul, so don't be afraid to allow others the same. The end result of all of this is to bring you to a more enlightened place, a more mindful state of being, a joyous outlook, a happier disposition, a sense of peace, balance, accomplishment, and feelings of fulfillment that allow you to be present in all areas of your life.

I hope this small book gave you the motivation you needed to embark on your own journey of discovery. I hope you enjoyed it and if you did, would you please leave a review so others feel inspired to read it as well?

Resources

Allen, D. (2015). *Getting Things Done: The Art of Stress-Free Productivity*. Penguin.

Stafford, R. M. (2017b). *Only Love Today: Reminders to Breathe More, Stress Less, and Choose Love*. Zondervan.

Turner, J. N. (2018). *Stretched Too Thin: How Working Moms Can Lose the Guilt, Work Smarter, and Thrive*. Revell.

Hollis, R. (2019). *Girl, Wash Your Face: Stop Believing the Lies about Who You Are So You Can Become Who You Were Meant to Be*.

Pacheco, D., & Pacheco, D. (2023, March 24). *Do Women Need More Sleep Than Men?* Sleep Foundation. https://www.sleepfoundation.org/women-sleep/do-women-need-more-sleep-than-men#:~:text=The%20average%20adult%20needs%20between,View%20Source%20%E2%80%94%20than%20men

Forman, T. (2019, April 11). *Self-Care Is Not An Indulgence. It's A Discipline. – Path Forward*. https://pathforward.org/self-care-is-not-an-indulgence-its-a-discipline/?gclid=CjwKCAjw_YShBhAiEiwAMomsEE2WokFLm03UKThozqk7c5k3LfLGe57TnjH5m1nfE6806MU0F6T4jxoCIG4QA vD_BwE

Staff, M. (2023, January 6). *What is Mindfulness?* Mindful. https://www.mindful.org/what-is-mindfulness/

Staff, M. (2022, October 4). *How to Practice Mindfulness.* Mindful. https://www.mindful.org/how-to-practice-mindfulness/

Intelligent Change. (n.d.). *Gratitude and Productivity Blog by Intelligent Change.* https://www.intelligentchange.com/blogs/read